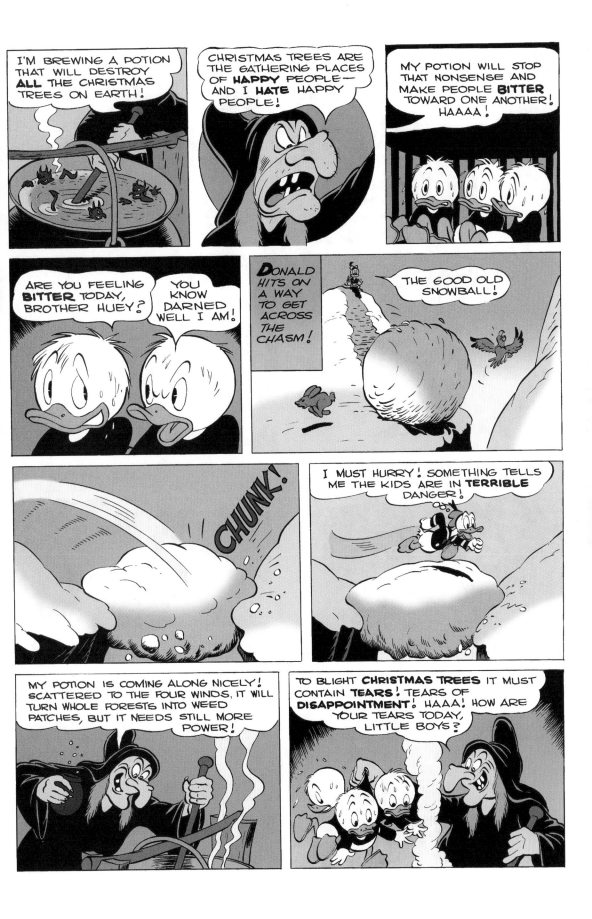

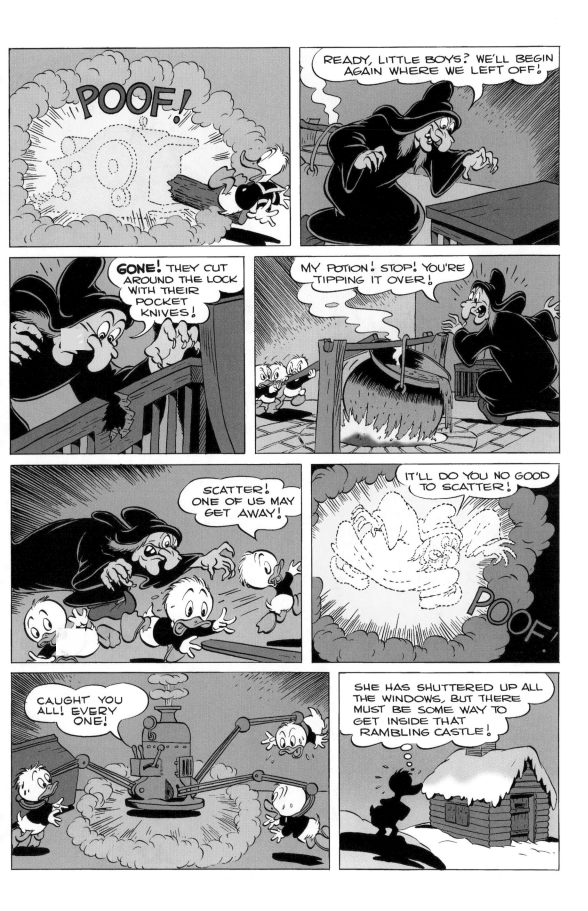

GEMSTONE PUBLISHING
presents
YOUR FAVORITE DISNEY COMICS

© 2005 Disney Enterprises Inc.

Delivered right to your door!

We know how much you enjoy visiting your local comic shop, but wouldn't it be nice to have your favorite Disney comics delivered to you? Subscribe today and we'll send the latest issues of your favorite comics directly to your doorstep. And if you would still prefer to browse through the latest in comic art but aren't sure where to go, check out the Comic Shop Locator Service at www.diamondcomics.com/csls or call 1-888-COMIC-BOOK.

FINALLY, THEY'RE HERE!

Walt Disney's
MICKEY MOUSE
meets
BLOTMAN

Is it possible that Mickey's life-long nemesis, The Phantom Blot, could be fighting on the side of law and order? Is it credible that Mickey would join forces with the Blot? And is it feasible that one of Mickey's closest friends is now an arch-fiend?

The answers to these questions can be found in Gemstone's latest special edition graphic novel, *Mickey Mouse Meets Blotman*. Forty-eight pages of nail-biting suspense for just $5.99 and on sale now. *Mickey Mouse Meets Blotman* is sure to become a classic.

So visit your local comic book store now and reserve your copy of *Mickey Mouse Meets Blotman*. If you need to find the location of a comic shop near you, call Diamond Comic Distributors' Comic Shop Locator service at 1-888-COMIC-BOOK. If there's no comic shop nearby, you may use the coupon below to order a copy, or order online at www.gemstonepub.com/disney.

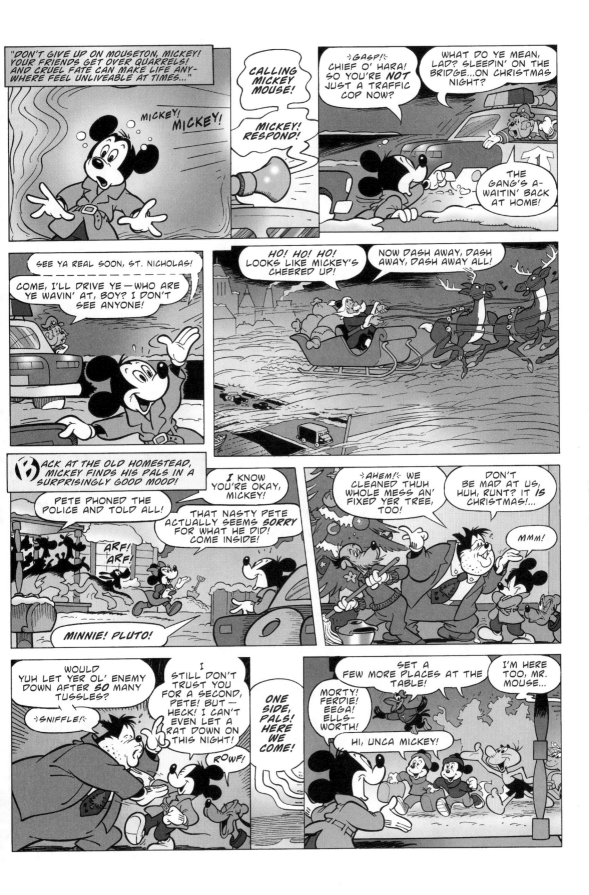

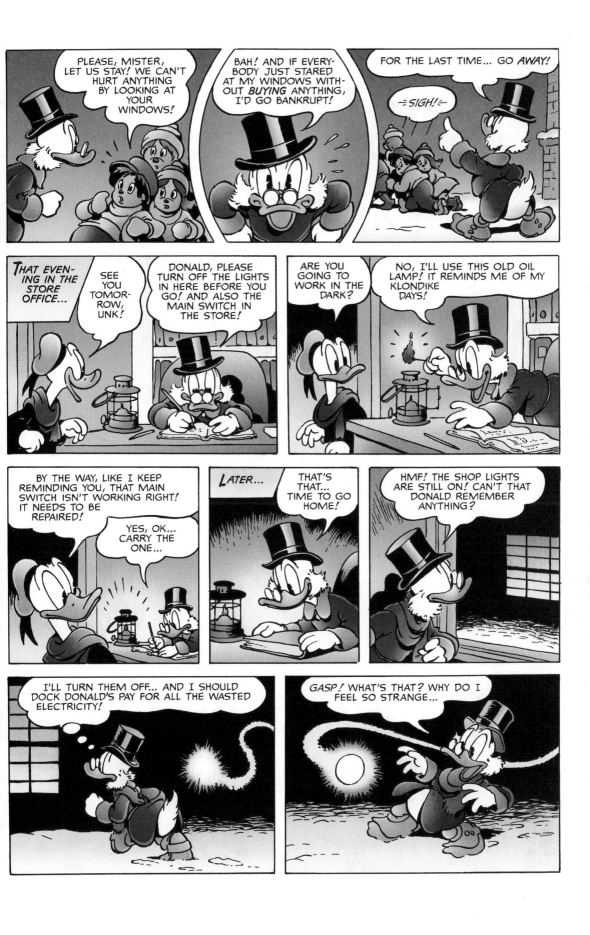

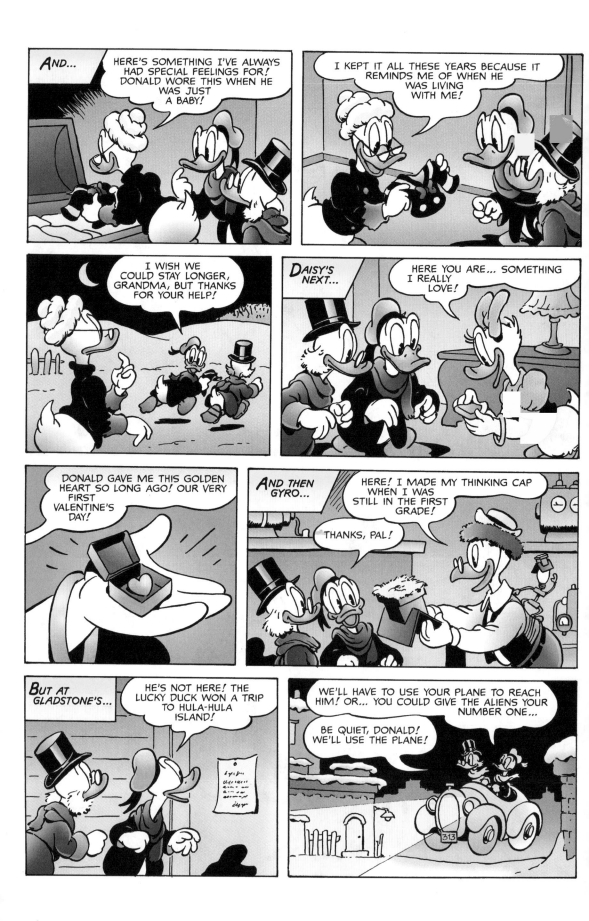

© 2005 Disney
Enterprises Inc.

The Life and Times of Scrooge McDuck by Don Rosa

We all wonder how Carl Barks' webfooted tycoon acquired his famous fortune—and in *Uncle Scrooge* 285-296 (1994-96), modern-day duck maestro Don Rosa told us in a legendary epic serial. From Scrooge's Scottish childhood to his worldwide quest for gold; from his ill-starred love life to his meetings with history's heroes, Rosa left no stone unturned, no penny unpinched. And now Gemstone Publishing is collecting all 12 Eisner-winning chapters in one 264-page trade paperback, annotated by Rosa himself and embellished with art never before seen in the United States. Look for it at your favorite book store or comic shop; at just $16.99, it's a deal even a tightwad could love.

But there's something wrong about all this, according to Pluto's figuring! Advance scouts for Santa wouldn't check on Grandma's cupcakes!

Cupcakes aren't even in Santa's department!

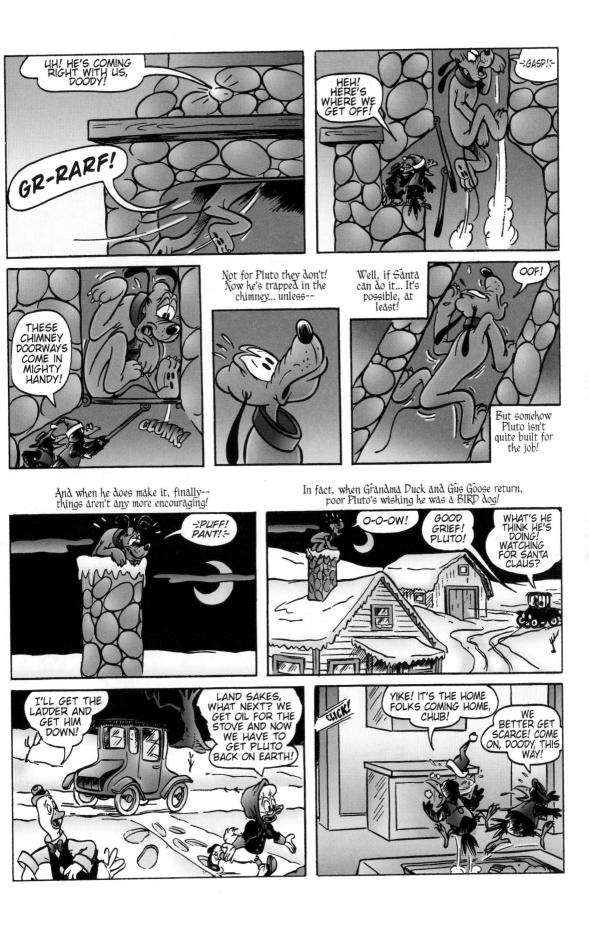

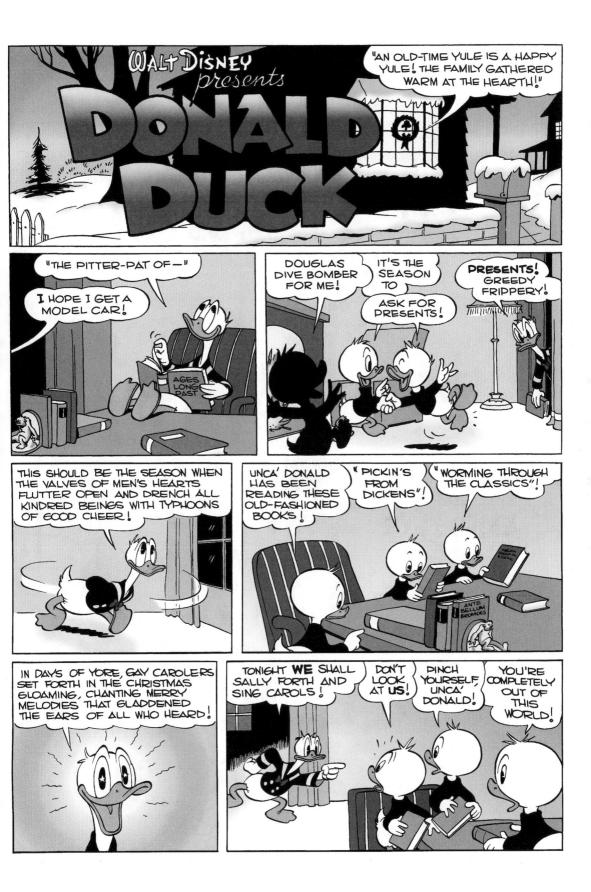

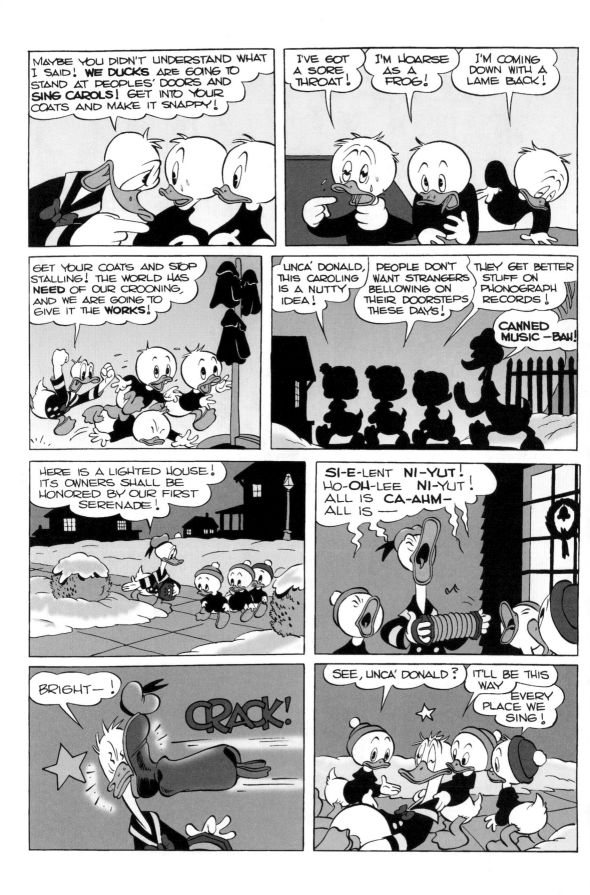

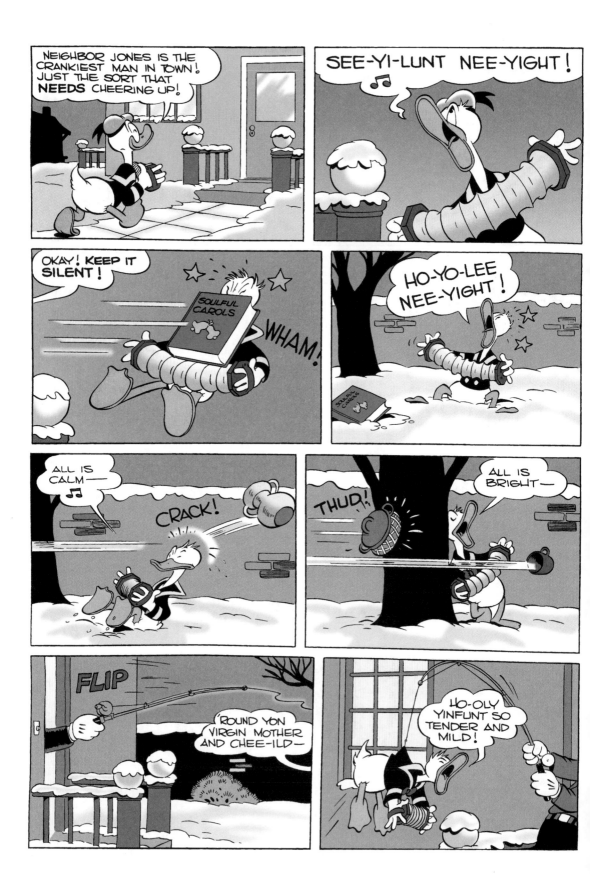

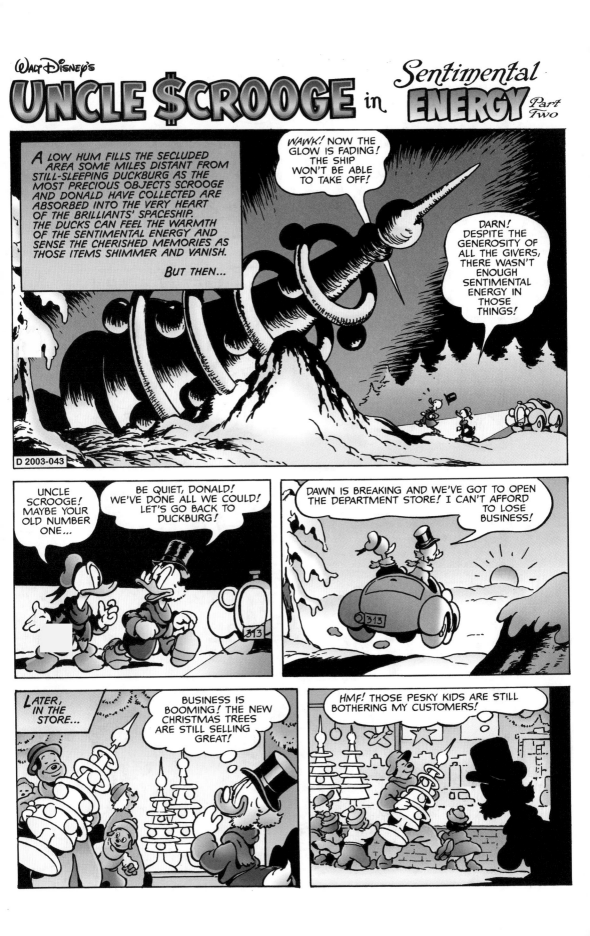